MÓNICA DE LA TORRE

THE HAPPY END / ALL WELCOME

ISBN 978-1-937027-73-5
Distributed in the USA by SPD/Small Press Distribution
Distributed in Canada via Coach House Books by Raincoast Books
Distributed in the UK by Inpress Books

First Edition, First Printing, 2017

Ugly Duckling Presse
The Old American Can Factory
232 Third Street, #E-303
Brooklyn, NY 11215

Cover image by Martino Gamper: "Black & Silver"
from the series *100 Chairs in 100 Days* (2005–2007)
Courtesy of Martino Gamper / Nilufar Gallery
Photography: Åbäke / Martino Gamper

Design by Don't Look Now! and d.p. menzimer
Typset in Caslon and Fort (a typeface by MCKL, a Los Angeles-based type
foundry and design studio run by Jeremy Mickel)

Printed and bound by McNaughton & Gunn, Saline, MI
Covers printed at Prestige Printing, Brooklyn, NY

The publication of this book is made possible in part by the National
Endowment for the Arts, by public funds from the New York City
Department of Cultural Affairs in partnership with the City Council, and
the continued support of the New York State Council on the Arts.

NYSCA

ART WORKS.

NYCULTURE

Mónica de la Torre

The Happy End / All Welcome

UGLY DUCKLING PRESSE
BROOKLYN, 2017

After Martin Kippenberger's installation "The Happy End of Franz Kafka's Amerika" *(an assortment of numbered tables and office desks with pairs of mismatched chairs within a soccer field flanked by grandstands) which references a giant job fair held by the Nature Theater of Oklahoma in Kafka's unfinished* Amerika—*a novel Kippenberger claimed never to have read.*

POSITIONS AVAILABLE

All are welcome!

Anyone who wants to become an artist should contact us!

Anyone who wants to be an artist, step forward!

We can make use of everyone, each in their place!

We have a place for everyone, everyone in their place!

Anyone thinking of their future belongs in our midst!

Anyone thinking of their future, your place is with us!

And we congratulate here and now those who have decided in our favor!

If you decide to join us, we congratulate you here and now!

— THE COMPANY

CAREER TRACK

Did you start off quietly at the very bottom and try to work your way up bit by bit?

Did you start off with a very small job and then work your way up by industry and application?

Did you start at an age in which the more advanced of your peers were almost ready to move on to better jobs?

Do you keep thinking that in their lives others have an advantage over you that you need to make up for with greater industry and a certain degree of self-denial?

Have you ever felt that your work hasn't, as you had hoped, turned out to be a prelude to some higher position, but rather that you've been pushed out of it into something even lower?

Have you felt that in comparison to a job you find repulsive, any other job would be welcome, and even a period of hunger and unemployment would be preferable to it?

Have you ever tried out every conceivable position for the sake of variety?

Think about it: Really, it isn't out of the question that you might be chosen and might one day sit as a worker at your desk and look out of your open window with no worries, for a while.

AVAILABLE POSITIONS

Sitting erect, pelvis curved out, cross-legged or with legs parallel.

Slumping, pelvis curved in.

Sitting erect, slightly leaning forward, resting elbows and arms on desk.

Reclining on chair, propping up feet on desk.

Sitting against back of chair, cross-legged or with legs parallel.

Plopped, arms over armrests, legs open wide.

Facing backward, with legs wrapping around back of chair.

Propped up by chair while standing.

Fast asleep, resting torso and arms on desk, with arms pillowing head.

Propping elbows on open book on desk, hands supporting forehead or smoothing out hair.

Plunked, head sunk into chest.

What is your position?

TABLE 20

BATHER:

If you can see what you can't see, does that mean you're seeing it?

ASPIRING LIFEGUARD:

I see shapes, not edges.

BATHER:

Meaning?

ASPIRING LIFEGUARD:

Meaning.

BATHER:

Astigmatism, you mean?

ASPIRING LIFEGUARD:

Nothing I can't just ignore.

BATHER:

There you go, getting everything confused again.

ASPIRING LIFEGUARD:

That's it; that's exactly it.

BATHER:

If you avert your eyes from something your eyes can't help but see, are you seeing it or not?

ASPIRING LIFEGUARD:

I see a nesting table in the distance. Table or tables? My vision is blurry at all distances. My corneas have flat and steep areas; likewise my mind.

BATHER:

Do you trust your other senses?

ASPIRING LIFEGUARD:

It depends on where I'm sitting.

BATHER:

Do you want the position or not?

VIEW FROM AN AERON CHAIR

A half-view of greenery, cut off by blinds.
Pinecones hanging in pairs, like testicles.
Brain balls, someone once said at a pool.
We were in it, looking up at a guy getting out.
This angle replicates that one, but the view
is more animated, less peopled.

The sky's changeups are reminders
that this will not drag on forever, despite
the ergonomic ease afforded by the seat
first devised for geriatric care, then stripped down.
It'd seem rational: if the elderly spent
their days in recliners, so could others,
dotcommers, say, properly incentivized.

And at least there is no symbolic logic
with eliminands and retinends.
No lasting premises either;
we will be priced out of any area.
No sooner than the conclusion is accepted
as consequent and part and parcel
of this universe of discourse, we'll come to realize
the sense in having new places to leave.

This is the chair's democracy.
Particularly this one, with its form-fitting mesh
forsaking foam and padding,
which cause overheating and cloud
the sitter's judgment.
It's recyclable, and that matters.

Still, the office chair's revolution is an oxymoron.

TABLE 17

RECRUITER:

How are you doing today?

WORKER:

I'm pretty board and I wanna play in theater.

RECRUITER:

How's your English?

WORKER:

My English is no good.

RECRUITER:

How do you mean?

WORKER:

My English is not very well.

My English is … no English.

My English is no where.

My English is not good and it is heard badly.

My English is no frequently.

My English is no native so apologies for everyone.

RECRUITER:

(She remembers the orientation session in which talent scouts were told to employ, at the drop of a hat, anyone whose use of language might increase activity in audiences' corrugator muscles or do the opposite, prompting zygomatic tension.)

Congratulations, you're hired.

SOURCES SOUGHT NOTICE

Solicitation Number: RFI-BPD-09-0028
Agency: Department of the Treasury
Office: Bureau of the Public Debt (BPD)

This is a sources sought notice and not a request for quotations. The purpose of this announcement is to seek qualified contractors with the capability to provide presentations for the Department of Treasury, Bureau of the Public Debt (BPD), and Management Meeting with experience in meeting the objectives as described herein. The Contractor shall conduct two three-hour programs that will discuss the power of humor in the workplace, the close relationship between humor and stress, and why humor is one of the most important ways that we communicate in business and office life and prevent burnout. Participants shall experience demonstrations of cartoons being created on the spot. The presenter shall refrain from using any foul language during the presentation. This is a business environment and we need the presenter to address a business audience.

TABLE 21

Index finger   left hand
frfv fvrf vrff vrrf rfvf rvff frrv frfvfrfv fvrf vrff vrff vffrf frfv f (1'6")

Index finger   right hand
jujm jumj muju ummj jumm jmuj umju jujm jujm jumj muju
ummj jujm j (35")

Index extended finger   right hand
hyhn hynh hnyh hynn hnyh ynnh hyhn hynh hnyh hynn hnyh
hnyh hyhn h (53")

Ring finger   right hand
Lol. Olo. Llo. . lol .lol lo.l lo.l lo.o lol. olo. Llo. .lol l (32")

All fingers   both hands
The practice of shorthand is very common in business working. (15")

COPY

Be accurate. Every conscioys error you make, slows up your
mental process and cuts down speed. (95 strokes, 28")

Keep your eyes on the copy. Every time you raise your etes
to see if you have made an error, you lose caluable seconds
examining the paper in uyour typewriter, and finding your
place again on the copy. (199 stroked, 35")

Sales letters are of two general types. First, the letter which is actually designed to sell as service or commodity. Secondly, the adjustment letter, which sells good will. Any library has good books on handling sales correspondence. A majority of such books, howeber, are written more for executives who head departments. The esult is that the busy secretary is discouraged from reading lengthy columns. The following simple and tested rules will suffice for daily office activities. The four aims of the sales letter are: attract attention: create desire: convince the mindl stimulate action. The four aims of the adjustment letter are: conciliate the reader; restate the facts; make reparation; conciliate again. To give your letters cgaracter, you should: take a personal attitude; adapt your letter to the reader's background, education or station in life; keep your temper; avoid scarcasm or witticisms; remind rather than instryct. Or, you can fgoret about these five points and summarize the principles into: "Be sincere." (1020 strokes–4', 28")

AD COPY

The girls in *The Happy End / All Welcome* make up a cast of recognizable characters, all ventriloquizing advertising copy and striving to be unique and desirable. Each gets their soliloquy: pinup secretaries, gamines, vamps, aspiring starlets, celebrity lookalikes, fashion hounds, compulsive eyebrow pluckers, shoe fetishists, thrift-store junkies, post-hippie hobos, and even ladies-who-lunch. Each rehearses a persona, offering a tenderly sardonic look at the art of fashioning oneself.

A mutable shape stating that downtime hasn't gone the way of the dodo.

Yet the days of sitting around seem extinct.

Now it's all go-go. No need to go into it; who doesn't know the feeling?

The dodo, maybe? Its temporality is other.

Its inability to adapt rendered it obsolete.

And so this prop here is adaptable as if to right evolutionary wrongs.

It encourages a certain flight, of the sitter's focus inward, when tilting back, and when sitting straight, to one's surroundings, an outrospection.

English?

Both ways must be had, or else …

All hinging on a lever and a handle, not as foolproof as the nod to Alice might lead you to believe.

Some groping under the seatback and trial and error is required.

And there's no how-to either. "The best way to explain it is to do it."

Feet on the ground, it's the drama of everyday living.

Feet up, it's the island of the mind, the dwelling place for other dodos whose existence only pictures and written accounts corroborate.

Change or die.

Who wants to go back to zero again?

QUESTIONNAIRE

DESCRIBE WHAT COLOR IS NOT

It's missing a thingness.

To the point of becoming, color camouflages supporting structures.

A vague interior finds in an exterior specific correlation.

Even if shapeless, it materializes in dabs, bursts, or blobs.

HOW MOOD-LIKE?

Like, I love that green.

Like, Benjamin Moore's color designers or 20-inch Indian human hair extensions.

Color resists paraphrase without metaphor.

Ruddiness says ripe, a want to be had.

Rose Quartz and Serenity were 2016's Official Pantone Colors of the Year.

Color is readymade sensation, emotion, feeling.

And/or.

A vague exterior finds in an interior specific correlation.

CAN IT BE ARTICULATED AS NARRATIVE?

As in red, white, and blue.

And *Untitled (USA Today)*.

An endless supply of candy wrapped in red, silver, and blue cellophane.

Flavors: cherry, pineapple, and Concord grape (the best tasting).

Tongue-cutting.

HOW DO WE KNOW HOW IT'S READ?

It's its own culture. White is one of my favorites. In the East it is associated with death.

Red nails once stood for status.

Now it's Be a Dahlia Won't You? The Thrill of Brazil, Yucatan
If U Want, I'm Not Really a Waitress.

Or the mimicking of natural nails.

HOW SIMULACRA?

To the point of becoming, color structures camouflage,
supporting it.

Buy Freedom Flags from just $1.60 each, all sizes in stock.

The celebrity/fitness guru has-been advises: "Make sure you get
all colors in your food. Your yellows, your purples, your reds,
your greens."

Disregard if you're a locavore.

When it comes down to it, some seasons come close to
monotonous.

Think potatoes. And snow.

TRUE OR FALSE?

No mode of excitement is absolutely colorless.

TABLE 25

CATERER:

Tell me a little about your background.

LINE COOK:

I was brought up to eat with my fork and knife, with my hands on the table instead of my feet like the Americans.

CATERER:

What's your favorite dish?

LINE COOK:

Social Pasta. I'm a believer in readymade flavor.

CATERER:

What's your philosophy in the kitchen?

LINE COOK:

I repurpose common leftovers, say, Parmesan cheese. Labor is a thing of the past. As an ingredient, especially if grated infrathin, Parmesan might be visible or invisible, non-retinal. It is used as an additive only less and less; now it is the base for dishes made with cheese rind stock. I repurpose common leftovers.

CATERER:

What's your favorite ingredient?

LINE COOK:

It's a tossup between eggs and butter. Butter is like letters: you can't make anything without it. And eggs are so versatile, they're the ultimate soft sculptures.

CATERER:

Of course, a huevo!

LINE COOK:

Say what?

CATERER:

For emphasis.

LINE COOK:

Justice hasn't been done to the egg. Warhol's already had the banana. An egg is white and flat, how can that be turned into a colored picture? If you turn it around this way and that, you'll come up with something.

Not in fetal position, curled in, but the opposite:
spread out, yet fully supported, encouraged, in fact,
to take any position imagined. What is one to desire
from a seated configuration? If audacity requires
averting devolution, a coming out of the shell.
The less prescribed the sitter's orientation turns,
the more the chair's potential unfolds, and the other way
around. Armrests easily serve as leg rests when reclining
on either side. The chair's open arms acquiesce to all:
slumping, varying degrees of verticality and horizontality,
legs extended, bent, tucked, or even in lotus position.
A permutational site; its backing unconditional.
With limbs reaching away from the ribcage, expanding
to the seatback's width, shoulders go down—
for equanimity, a formula. What a progressive view
of parenting! Just enough protection; harnessing
the body, yet prodding it beyond conformity's threshold.

TABLE 45

The Human Resources Manager interviews a candidate for the position of Armchair Psychologist or Pop Freudianist.

During the first part of the interview the applicant is asked to work on various case studies by interpreting the dreams of different subjects.

The second part of the interview involves discussing the development of an app for users to log dreams that might eventually be reenacted. These could fall under five broad categories:

Status Panic

Masochistic Ideations Posing as Sadistic Fantasies

Total Disconnect

Catastrophic Fear of the Collapse of Self

Teeth Dreams

CASE STUDY

In a vast, sun-filled market with large windows and a view of the water, reminiscent of some place in Seattle or San Francisco that the subject has never visited, there is a baker's stall displaying hearty-looking loaves with reliefs of words on them. The subject tries to read one: it could say either PAN or PAIN, but the loaf is cut in half and only a portion of the word is legible. The next day the subject goes back to the market, and asks the baker what a new loaf says. He answers it spells HUNGER. Or was it HOMBRE, or HAMBRE? The subject cannot recall.

CASE STUDY

At a party in a country clubhouse, all the food and drink is placed on tables that are impossibly tall, way out of reach above people's heads, so as to keep bugs away. It seems normal to all the guests present.

A subject dreams that Karen Finley is recounting an old performance of hers in which she exposed her collaborator, a respected poet, to exploitive sexual acts. Finley pulled her on a leash as they traversed a series of linked spaces, as if they were on a train. The subject compares the sequence Finley describes so vividly to the passage through different cars in the sci-fi film *Snowpiercer*.

Suddenly the performance is happening. The subject has joined it. The poet is reclined on an examination table, naked, her legs spread next to a pair of scissors and some bottled liquids. The subject takes one of them and squeezes it near the poet's vagina. A distinct scent of ammonia pierces the air. The subject realizes it's a hair removal product. "Why would you do that to me?" the poet asks. Whether or not there were any spectators contemplating the scene is a question left open.

The subject cannot recall what Finley's exploits were. A line was crossed. Finley admits to her feelings of guilt. The subject identifies. Next, Finley talks about how forgiving and broad-minded the poet has always been. The poet by then has morphed into a man to whom the subject feels worrisomely attracted. He is now a server at a trendy New York City restaurant. He married Finley after the performance, but the marriage didn't last. He has been married to three other women since and is currently unavailable.

While still dreaming, the subject marvels at the scrambled temporality of her dream.

CASE STUDY

Husband and wife are in bed, each with their respective corpses. These are benign, lifeless, hollow bodies, which makes them appealing to the mice nesting inside them.

The subject's dream is heavy with dread. Even though both corpses are stuffed with mice, the husband's has just been cut open. Will the rodents now hide all over the house? Will the noise they make with their unremittingly growing incisors interrupt the silence of the night?

What if they zip up the husband's dead body to contain the mice and then release them out into the woods? This raises the troublesome possibility that the subject won't be able to go outside anymore without fearing that they creep up on her.

CASE STUDY

On the first day of a new job, after quitting a highly desirable one, the subject experiences genuine befuddlement when asked to contribute $20 for a colleague's taxi fare from the airport.

The day's obligations include putting documents in boxes and loading them into a coworker's trunk. It soon becomes apparent that the subject occupies the lowest rung of the bureaucracy and that, other than this odd version of paperwork, there is nothing of consequence at stake.

Find the exact "seconds time" that each word is sung in the song.

Please tell us parenting advice for India.

Judge a user's privacy preference.

Provide a similar word or phrase.

Find photographs of judges.

Order Tagalog for English translations by their quality.

How relevant is this job result compared to the job query?

Watch videos and click buttons.

Mark the ball as it leaves the player's hands.

Find email addresses and names of owners or general managers of
gyms.

Tell us how you perceive an image, an interesting short survey.

Estimate gender and age of faces.

Judge the sentiment expressed toward users' experience with care
provided.

Find department chairs.

Extract information from a table.

VIEW FROM AN UTRECHT CHAIR

What's to simplify forms? Two half rectangles perform
as armrests and front legs. No hind legs
prop up the back. A play on angles:
another identical half rectangle, yet generously cushioned, acts
as seat and back. Its structure shows sideways.
It would be out of place in offices
or institutional lounges. It's too quirky, too easy.
Its low height wouldn't lead to any deliverables,
only shameless idling. It is no site
for escapism, though. Deep and narrow, it'd prove
hard to get up out of, for some.
Plus, designed for higher latitudes, it stores presence-

asserting heat. A pair, however, would elevate a
familiar conversation setting and might lead to stationary
drifting. Its original upholstery was sailcloth after all.
With the exuberance of visible stitches, it says,
"I have been assembled. I traffic in utopias,
in the zigzag rhythms of colors and geometries."
In a corner of the room, almost overlooked—
its side view hindered by a bed stand—
had it not been for the rub-off
of controlled conditions of display in a studio
where the designer's clean, cantilevered, and primary-colored designs
waver between receiving the body and the gaze.

Assistant Director *(through megaphone):*

Call for Feeling Manufacturers!
Use color to shape the
public's emotions, add a
little jingle, and bingo!

Three people sitting on a tandem bench come forth.

Each applicant is assigned a color around which to improvise lyrics for jingles.

Only found language displayed in the color assigned to each can be used.

Applicants are given two hours to go searching for text in the city.

The Assistant Director selects corresponding loops from the Buddha Machine 2.0, a portable music player, as accompaniment.

BLUE

service changes

                for more information please call
          delta

clean air
       hybrid

electric air
          electric hybrid

retail hybrid
                  space available

       for more information please call
dry cleaners

mechanical voice
      available

it's free
   hybrid

air stream   it's free   let's celebrate

integrated
     ambulance

integrated

        police

              metro hybrid

VOICE

           it's free

mechanical voice

           available

let's celebrate

           better rates

new

        friendly

              coin-operated

commuter
& service

        air stream

           service changes

        stream air

           change services

        change air

           stream services

stream change

        air services

change stream

        service air

stream services

        air changes

(Loop 7: commanding, slightly menacing)

Private property
Do not lean
Between cars
Do not lean

Exit
99 cent paradise

The next stop is
Outside of the subway is dangerous
Billiards and bar

It is a violation
To ride or walk

Help us keep the subway clean &
Get over it!
Ask the station agent for your litter free ATM

Yeah yeahs

Hats, games, gags, and magic
Are subject to random search
Exit

Masters of masquerade : Get over it!
Exit

Make-up, wigs, health food
Three hour photo
Ask the station agent for respect

Ask the station agent for your
LOFT for rent
99 cent Paradise
Emergency exit only

If you drop something don't go
Ask the station agent for
your safety

Emergency exit only

(Loop 9: high-pitched, shrill)

Dolls: where family fun is no illusion
                              A new competition reality series

Where construction fraud is no illusion

                                        FREE

Wage or other labor violations

                                        FREE

Unsafe policies and conditions

Where employee misconduct is no illusion

                                        FREE

False disability and injury claims
Where contractor and vendor fraud is no illusion
Where theft of MTA property is no illusion

Too much debt?

Divorce or family court?

Inefficiencies and waste of money?

                                        FREE

Watch and jewelry

Payment plans, FREE consultation

Special offer!

Call!   Mail!

   Big Blue Wizard

Lottery

               Clean up after your dog

               ZING ZANG ZOOM!

          Ringling Bros. and Barnum & Bailey

             Where illusion is family fun.

Assistant Director (*screams into a megaphone*):

Anybody else? One
more, with feeling!

A random passerby who fancies himself a game changer joins in.

ORANGE

Dance the Orange. Paint dripping like the juice from an
Orange. Orange is yellow and paint dripping like the juice
from an Orange. And red combined. Orange is color and
Orange is yellow and fruit. And Orange is yellow and fruit
combined. Orange tastes like a splash of color in a splash of
color the mouth. Orange is color and fruit. Orange brightens
space without warming it up. Orange brightens optical effect
without warming it up.

Assistant Director (*hollering*):

Rate the performance. Did the previous works match the color they have been assigned? Did blue feel blue? Red made you feel _____. If yellow gave you anxiety, please contact The Company's Management.

FURNITURE TESTER

She goes around the floor jotting notes on the chairs she sits in.

From each one her outlook is somewhat different.

The views gleaned from each are not in concert.

She has an overall picture, but it's about to implode. Is this what people mean by "creative disruption"?

She would like to devote herself to whatever best fits her skill set.

If she stays put long enough, could she hope for an improved past, she wonders.

Yet mostly her approach is a tourist's, however much she applies herself.

You don't always have to return the favor, she realizes.

In general she's not a verbalizer.

She mainly hears herself listening to, or all too often, uttering malapropisms, sometimes eagerly.

Given the vagueness of her records—has her experience been built into the design? are the stimuli interior or exterior?—she considers tinnitus as metaphor.

Yet what she gets from sitting for hours on end is tendinitis in the hip.

She goes on seeking comfort in uncomfortable chairs.

YES OR NO

A dead office is overhead.

A living office is an organism.

.

YES OR NO

Early open-plan offices are called office landscapes
    (*Bürolandschaften*).

The landscape's design appears chaotic,
    emulating Italian baroque gardens.

Furniture in office landscapes is placed at odd angles.

Plants and a few partitions divide personnel
    according to genera and work flow.

Entrepreneurs contemplate the landscape.

Partitions need less maintenance than plants.

So that personnel can move around and up and down
    and function as vertical machines,
    office landscapes are sectioned into action offices.

It is suboptimal to give vertical machines space to move
    around and up and down.

Flexible offices are not cost-effective.

Furniture in action offices is placed orthogonally.

Plants are replaced by partitions on three sides.

Action offices become cubicles.

Action offices become dead offices.

Plants enliven offices in pictures.

Living offices are safe environments for plants.

Dead offices attract those for whom work is unnatural compared to play or rest.

Living offices attract those for whom work is as natural as play or rest.

Individuals in dead offices are workers.

Individuals in living offices are human performers.

Workers work for higher-ups.

Human performers work to satisfy their higher-level egos.

"Bees are not natural and that is natural enough."

YES OR NO

If unchecked, workers dillydally to slow down operations.

When workers have unexpected collisions
    in hallways or restrooms,
    they tend to linger and disturb others.

When human performers have unexpected collisions
    in previously designated areas, they have
    serendipitous encounters leading to collaborations.

When workers talk about the weather
    or compliment each other's clothing,
    they are dawdling.

When human performers talk about the weather
    or compliment each other's clothing,
    they are being creative.

YES OR NO

In action offices, vertical machines
 (also known as knowledge workers)
 confer, negotiate, plan, direct, read, take notes, write,
 draw, trace blueprints, calculate, dictate, telephone,
 punch cards, type, multigraph, record,
 and check at freestanding units.

Workers whose tasks demand that they hardly get up
 from their freestanding units
 are also known as slouching machines.

In living offices, human performers
 (also known as members of the creative class)
 chat, converse, co-create, divide and conquer, huddle,
 show and tell, warm up and cool down, process
 and respond, contemplate, and create at workstations
 and work points.

Those who receive no compensation for tasks
 that include plan, read, take notes, write, draw, calculate,
 telephone, type, chat, converse, co-create, huddle, show
 and tell, warm up and cool down, process and respond,
 contemplate, and create are known as the unemployed.

YES OR NO

In living offices work points include jump spaces.

Jump spaces are not landings.

Landings are perch spots adjacent to meeting spaces
    and forums where human performers can interact.

Neither workers nor the unemployed perch in jump spaces.

Neither workers nor the unemployed tweet at perch spots.

Neither workers nor the unemployed jump in landings.

The unemployed may perch, tweet, and jump wherever they please.

Repositionable furniture belongs in forums.

Open discussions occurring at forums are focused.

Open unfocused discussions do not take place in plazas.

Plazas are welcoming public spaces at highly trafficked areas
of the work environment.

Parking lots are not plazas.

Elevators are not plazas.

Restrooms are not plazas.

Water-cooler areas are plazas.

Plazas have amenities as points of attraction.

Plazas invite individuals to mix, mingle, and shop.

When human performers shop, they are engaged in
a recreational community-building activity.

Shopping is productive.

Overproduction is not productive.

AD COPY

The customer is always right and let the latest installment of the polyphonic, sprawling *The Happy End / All Welcome* be the proof of the pudding. No longer the passive, voiceless victims of draconian capitalist forces, consumer culture allows us to exercise the subjectivity we've been granted via interpolation (see Barbara Kruger's "I shop therefore I am") by talking back to the machine. Disaffected consumers of the world, unite!™

VIEW FROM A FOLDING CHAIR

Never decorative, it embodies a chair's provisional character.

Utilitarian, never just there, called upon to serve.

Communal, egalitarian, leveling its occupants, gathered for an occasion.

Rarely will it hold the sitter captive. Its precariousness invites walkouts, even when the seat is secured by an admittance fee.

Repositionable, it favors assorted geometries of attention: the frontal and single-focused, the shifting and radial.

Irreverent, whether in an institutional setting or not, signaling reversible orders.

Possibly carnivalesque, displaying an upside-down world, as in:

> a projection of the high-desert landscape and transit
> 　　surrounding an old ice plant in the desert
> requiring no other technology but a lens and a dark room;
> ironically inverted in this picture of a tiny fraction of the
> 　　planet—
> with no search engine logo and copyright date camouflaged
> 　　to appear like a wisp of a stratus cloud—
> is the electrical plant across the street
> grids reversed, as is the soundtrack, extemporaneously
> 　　produced

by the cars and pickup trucks seen fleeting by from east to
west though by the sound we know they're going west
to east, and vice versa;

a projection within a projection

these are moving images to experience, but not keep.

Unsung, stacked, piled against a wall, or hidden in closets,
folding chairs will be counted on again since, plastic palace
people, they're both transience and ritual.

Welcome into the fold. Who cares what the future brings.

TABLE 7

Seeking a potential Spiritualist to conduct regular assessments of The Company's psychic abilities, particularly in the realms of:

Automatic writing

Channeling

Dowsing

Precognition

Multilocation

Remote viewing

Retrocognition

Second sight

As part of the application process, a potential Spiritualist consults the I Ching as well as Xul Solar's visionary writings and paintings, digging into their sources.

LIMITATIONS AND CONSTRAINT

inthenexttiertheyadorehimnotasheisnolongerhumaninthenexttier
theyadorehimasanibisforapparentlywidelydifferentthingsmental
cloudsofahomogeneousbasisfromhomogeneityemergesheterogeneity
accompaniedtoobylampstypicalofwisdomitselasticfreneticclouds
noncloudslimitationsarepitifulinthenexttierheisadoredasagoat
aspanordionysuseffectiveregardlesssuchisthistendencyofmodern
thoughtinthenexttierheisadoredasagoldenhawkitswingstheskysun
andmoonitseyesenduringglimmersinthenexttierheisadoredasacrab
anamuletofcomplicatedcolorseverythingoftenaccompaniedthosein
theoutertieradorehimasamanoffreneticspiritualcloudsgoingback
archaicideasinthenexttierheisadoredasaramitsfleecewrapsidols

forathousandyearstheylivedsidebyside
downriverthrivezooecologicalcolonies
livetrunksfinaldesirablethingstoeach
theirownlikewaterandoilandwinethisis
thefirstfundamentalaxiomsymbolizedby
finiteintelligencesodonotbringtolight
productsofcriticismthesecretdoctrine
isametaphysicalearthreceptivetoother
thingswithsimilardesireshowwherethey
gathercoexistforcenturiesinsuchtimes
yououghtnotinterferewiththepractices
ofothersandclinglikefireitisthetiers
wheretheydogatherbecomingoneabsolute
beinganimalcolonieswhereeverythingis
twinedtheholytrinitytruncatedknotted

returnedtohisprimordialelementthestatueshallbeoverthrown
equivalenttomineandmynotimycounterstatueandmynonrequired
notiwhichevenicannotfindremainingstillthemountainwhenthe
wholeuniversenecessarilyfilledtheinfiniteallwithdarkness
thereisnoeyetoperceivelightthatmybeingmightbeestablished
andcontinuethereitcouldnotfindhaveisentintotheworldthati
whowouldbemyequivalentwhoparticipatesinbusinessaftereons
ofmultiplyingintheskiesfromwhichhungtheruinsofcitiesonto
whichfireclungandtheruinsofcitiesbelowtherewasnocenterno
luminosityonlylyingspiritscelestialequivalentsandnobodys
businessfastasleepinadeepslumbermynotinotmycounterstatue

o n e m e r e g l a n c e o f m i n e a n n i h i l a t e s t h o s e
w h o i n f l a t e a n d d e f l a t e t h e m s e l v e s e a r t h
r e c e p t i v e o n f r e e c o m p r e h e n s i o n d e p e n d s
a n d r e a p i n g p e o p l e a s i f t h e y w e r e s c y t h e s
w i t h u g l y a n t i n o m i e s a n d f a c e l e s s l i q u i d
a m i d t i t a n i c t o r s o l e s s e n t i t i e s o f h u m a n
m a s s e s o f t e n p l e a s u r i n g e a c h o t h e r w h i l e
t h e y d i r e c t t h e i r d a m a g e w h i c h d i s p e r s e s
o r a c c u m u l a t e s a n d t h e p e r u s a l o f t h e w o r k
i t s e l f t h e r e f o r e n o a p o l o g y w i l l r e q u i r e
t o a s k t h a t r e a d e r s d i r e c t t h e i r c o b w e b b y
d a m a g e t e a r e a c h o t h e r s f l o a t i n g m e m b e r s
a c c u m u l a t i n g a w a r s t a t e a s t a t e o f w a r n o w
i t i s w r i t t e n s o a n u n d e r s t a n d i n g f o l l o w s
s u c h a g e n e r o u s g i f t a l o o s e m e m b e r f l o a t s
t a n g l e d i n f l i g h t m o r e t h a n n i g h t a s g u i d e
c o u r t e s a n s a r e f e w i n n u m b e r i n s u c h z o n e s
t h r o w i n g z i g z a g g i n g t h u n d e r b o l t s b a s i c
i d e a s b e f o r e e n t e r i n g t h e t a l l c o l l a p s e s
c a n n o t f i n d c a n n o t m a k e h i m s e l f f a m i l i a r
m e a n w h i l e t h e y t a k e p l e a s u r e i t i s b e y o n d
h e l l i s h t h e n i g h t t h e d o w n f a l l s n u m e r o u s
m a n m a s s e s e n t a n g l e d i n i n t e r n e c i n e w a r s
a n d r e a p i n g p e o p l e a s i f t h e y w e r e s c y t h e s

66 The credentials you provided cannot be determined to be authentic.

TABLE 41

*A Consultant discusses her vision for
The Company's Strategic Plan with the
Company Manager. She sits before a
lab table with five different body or-
gans preserved in jars of formaldehyde.*

COMPANY MANAGER:

You said organizations should function like
a living organism. Might you take a look
at these organs and explain to us which
functions of theirs can be applied to
company hierarchy?

CONSULTANT:

Here they're nearly disfigured by death and
pickling fluid! You wouldn't want that in an
organization. If preservation is your priority,
what you'll get is atrophy and inhibited
growth.

COMPANY MANAGER:

Of course. How about you identify the
organs and take it from there?

CONSULTANT:

In this jar you have the amygdala, after

which Human Resources Management should be modeled. It is the brain's fear center, regulating reward and punishment systems or, to give it a positive spin, motivation. It processes negative thoughts and irritability at violations of personal space. Its size correlates to individuals' creative thinking and emotional intelligence. It's mind-blowing that such a small part of the brain would be responsible for the Big Five personality traits, you know? OCEAN, or CANOE, depending on whether you'd like to be in the water, fully immersed in it, or on it, peacefully crossing over it.

COMPANY MANAGER:

Please, in the interest of time ...

CONSULTANT:

Yes, sorry. As the regulator of emotional responses, the amygdala determines feelings of interconnectedness as much as HRM shapes the staff's identification with the company. To the point: strategic incentives keep the staff happy. Everything from Muzak to 24-hour gyms, espresso bars, free snacks, field trips, community gardens, retreats, bonuses, you name it, the ability to BYOD, makes a big difference. Not only will staffers get the job done, they will also be nicer to their colleagues, which will reduce hostility and apprehension in the workplace.

COMPANY MANAGER:

The organ is glowing in the jar.

CONSULTANT:

It must be over-stimulated. You'll want to make sure your staff members have outlets for their drives. Otherwise the risk is that they suffer an amygdala highjack and become violent.

COMPANY MANAGER:

What do you suggest?

CONSULTANT:

It would be my honor to devise a business plan for your company that meets everyone's needs. For that, I would conduct private interviews with your staffers. There is no one-size-fits-all solution, especially when it comes to something as personal as sublimation. I mean, ultimately that's what is at stake.

COMPANY MANAGER:

Mind you, the clock is ticking.

Next we have the hippocampus, which
is responsible for forming long-term
memories. Archivists should function as
efficiently as the hippocampus does. Often
what we think is worth archiving isn't worth
the effort in the long run, and what we toss
turns out to be valuable. We wonder too
if the mere fact of not having something
any longer is precisely what bestows on it
mysterious value. But if we hesitate, we end
up hoarding.

A healthy hippocampus makes no such
mistakes. If every stimuli received, every
thought and sensation ever had, were
consciously taken into account every second
of our waking lives, how would we function?
Remembering can be a time suck. Ah, but
the hippocampus is wise and ruthless in
its selectivity. To think of the countless
minutiae it relegates to the trash heap
minute by minute!

COMPANY MANAGER:

Who tracks the archivists' work?

CONSULTANT:

You entrust the archive with articulating
the company's history the same way you
entrust your hippocampus with your own

declarative memory. You don't question what's forgotten; for the most part you can't even remember it.

Next we have a thumb. Hard to tell if a male or a female's, but in evolutionary terms, it matters little. It is a simple yet complex matter. The power and precision grips gave us countless advantages over other species. When we became bipeds, our hands were freed from the demands of walking on all fours. Having opposable thumbs allowed us to swing clubs and throw rocks at our opponents.

All business strategies, to succeed, need to have a firm grasp of these principles. What are a company's prehensile activities? How can rivals be kept at bay?

COMPANY MANAGER:

Not by clubbing them, I hope!

CONSULTANT:

Not at all. The rule of thumb is: Shun primitive behavior, welcome primitive impulses.

What do we have here in this next jar? Aha! The pea-sized pituitary gland. Excellent. Think of it as managers across the chain of command overseeing the company's daily workflow, its metabolism and production rhythms, its growth and sustainability. Above all is the CEO in a Turkish seat. That's a joke, by the way. The pituitary is enclosed in a bone-like case called the *sella turcica*. Why not have one built, actually? It could be a powerful symbol, lest a staffer forget where the buck stops.

COMPANY MANAGER:

Interesting, but surely you understand our company. We don't really have a CEO. We have an Artistic Director. The office chairs surrounding us are ghosts of obsolete hierarchies. We keep them as reminders of what can go wrong.

CONSULTANT:

There could not be a better segue to the next organ, the pineal gland. Look at it! A gorgeous, if a bit deformed, pinecone.

COMPANY MANAGER:

So what about it?

CONSULTANT:

It has no double. No left and right. If there's an Artistic Director, there's one only, with a non-fungible vision. And if his or her vision is fungible, you don't want it lodged at the center of the cranium. This gland regulates circadian rhythms, delicately balancing wakeful hours and sleep, awareness and dreams.

It is the missing link between the physical and spiritual worlds. Every night it coaxes us into surrendering control and venturing into the luminous darkness or the dark luminosity of our dream world —depending on whether you're a glass-half-full or a glass-half-empty kind of person. Disposition does not concern us, however; predisposition does.

I am no Theosophist, I subscribe to rational, positive views, but if for Mme. Blavatsky the pineal gland was the third eye, for Descartes it was "the principal seat of the soul." I got that from Wikipedia. Doesn't it sound nice? It makes you wonder how many seats Descartes thought the soul had.

VIEW FROM A MANAGEMENT CHAIR

With the information on hand, impossible to discern
    the cubicle's wood.
Without question it's an honest material; it's just that
    the online database,

with digital images and descriptions of various types, magnifies,
without much reliability, it seems, the differences in their grains.

With no basis except for its blondeness, in such issues
    a received knower,
without ever before having considered the matter, the guess

with regard to the source genus is that it's oak, birch, or hard maple.
Without any of those trees being native to the region, though, it's
    up in the air.

With nothing else competing for the retina's attention,
without any visual input other than the panels' loopy growth rings,

with only a keyboard in sight, a lamp, a flower-patterned
    tissue box, and scraps,
without being a dendrochronologist, time is the one thing
    to manage.

The Problem of Labor + A Theory of Distraction. Walter Benjamin: *Selected Writings, Volume 3: 1935–1938*. Attempt to determine the effect of the work of art once its power of consecration has been eliminated. Parasitic existence of art based on the sacred. Fashion is an indispensable factor in the acceleration of the process of becoming worn out. Technology is an indispensable factor in the acceleration of the process of becoming worn out. The values of distraction should be defined with regard to film, just as the values of catharsis are defined with regard to tragedy. The values of distraction should be defined with regard to. Distraction and destruction as the subjective and objective sides, respectively, of one and the same process. The relation of distraction to absorption should be examined. The survival of artworks should be represented from the standpoint of their struggle for existence. Their true humanity consists in their unlimited adaptability. The criterion for judging the fruitfulness of their effect is the communicability of this effect. The Greeks had only one form of (mechanical) reproduction: minting coins. They could not reproduce their artworks, so these had to be lasting. Hence: eternal art. Just as the art of the Greeks was geared toward lasting, so the art of the present is geared toward becoming worn out. *The Practice of Everyday Life*. *La perruque* is the worker's work disguised as work for his employer. The applicant checks emails once more finding nothing of particular note. At 240 wpm you are an oral reader. You can make progress by suppressing subvocalization. It may be as simple a matter as a secretary's writing a love letter on "company time" or as complex as a cabinetmaker's "borrowing" a lathe to make a piece of furniture for his living room.

Under different names in different countries this phenomenon is becoming more and more general, even if employers "penalize" it or "turn a blind eye" on it in order not to know about it. The worker who indulges in *la perruque* actually diverts time from the factory for work that is free, creative, and precisely not directed toward profit. Advanced search. Play the game of free exchange. Please read: a personal appeal from Wikipedia founder Jimmy Wales. Freeze-frame Baroque. This phrase was used to describe the work of someone whom the applicant cannot remember. Receives a Google alert on a namesake's Twitter. Deletes spam for Viagra. Deletes a Facebook alert. At 400 wpm you are an auditory reader who can practice in order to break the sound barrier. Checks emails. Confirms friend on Facebook. Removes tags of family photos. A stranger sends new friend request. Deletes invitation to a 60th birthday celebration of someone who wouldn't know who the applicant is if she showed up at the party. Deletes Facebook alert of a reply to a thread deleted earlier today. Deletes email announcing that no documentaries will be screened that night, but that you can buy a ticket to a fictitious screening if you want to make a donation. Adds item to list of to dos. Looks up definition of "aughts." At 1,000 wpm you are a visual reader, your reading speed is the gem of your cv.

66 This screen is so small i keep hitting things that take me to the wrong places.

AD COPY

Self-documenting as both code and self-recording craze,
preemptive of its own critique. Not Cartesian but Trecartian:
I record, therefore I am. The poems in *The Happy End / All
Welcome* start in medias res, no establishing shots for context.
Enter the slash: *and* as well as *or* and line break. As in
voyeurism / exhibitionism / numbered exhibits. It's not just
poetry. Is poetry not just—? Thanks for asking.

TABLE 12

A Headhunter at the hunting blind at the edge of the field keeps an eye on a middle-aged potbellied man in oversized underwear who eerily resembles Martin Kippenberger. He's about to get in a full-size Barbie tub near a couple of lifeguard chairs, holds a cigarette in one hand and a hard-boiled egg in the other.

In the Headhunter's estimation, this man could be either rapt in thought or overhearing the interview between the Bather and the Lifeguard next to him. He might also be reminiscing on the teepee villages at American Western theme campsites he stayed at in the old days with friends, which always had hot tubs.

The Headhunter wonders if he is seeking employment—why else would he be at the fair? He cannot begin to imagine what position might be appropriate for this individual defying categorization, whose insouciance clashes with the professional aspirations of the fairgoers.

An idea comes to him in a flash: this man could play the Unhappy Hedonist!

QUESTIONNAIRE FOR PROSPECTIVE CHAIN SMOKER

I. Do you smoke?

II. —Why do you?
—Where do you?
—When do you?
—How often do you in a day?
—Do you more at certain times of the day?
    —every day?
    —alone?
    —with others?
    —more when alone or when with others?
—Who are the others?
—Do you around your family?
    —around kids?
    —have kids?
    —live with kids?
—When were you born?
—Where were you born?
—When did you start?
—While you were growing up, were you allowed to in the house?
    —did your parents?
    —your siblings?
        —parents with you?
        —siblings with you?
        —you alone?
        —love your parents?
    —your parents tell you it was bad?
—Why did you start?

—With whom did you start?
—Do you offer yours to others?
—Who are the others?
—Are there any in your pocket?
—What kind are in your pocket?
—Do you prefer lights?
    —water colors or oils?
    —woods or the beach?
    —salt or sugar?
    —ring dings or yodels?
        —or kale?
    —pencils or pens?
—Do you drink?
    —more when you drink?
    —have sex?
    —more after you have sex?
    —with others after you have sex?
—Do you have trouble breathing?
    —with restraint?
    —stopping?
—Do you have a chosen faith?
    —fun?
—How often do you feel guilty?
    —think about death?
—Do you prefer the sky or the sea?
    —staccato or legato?
—Do you have a lot of friends?
    —fun?
—Have you done things like this before?
—What is the best way to reach you?

MORE AVAILABLE POSITIONS

Perched awkwardly atop the edge of a seat of an upside-down armchair whose backrest leans on a briefcase on top of a pile of papers on the ground.

Sitting on the backrest of an upside-down armchair leaning on a briefcase on top of a pile of papers on the ground, arms slung over armrests, nape reclined on the seat that serves as back.

Hugging the seat of an upside-down armchair whose backrest leans on a briefcase on top of a pile of papers on the ground, pelvis turning outward, right foot on the ground for support, and left knee bent toward seat serving as back.

Sitting sideways in an armchair, legs draping over armrest.

Lying on the seat of an armchair with legs up against the backrest.

Sitting cross-legged in an armchair, head leaning back, unfolded newspaper covering head.

VIEW FROM A LOUNGE CHAIR

in the posture afforded by birch and the phantom of wartime

    a black, new-moon sky would turn the ocean

surplus parachute straps, latticed

    invisible; in the print it glimmers in moonlight

to form the seat and back, hurtled into indeterminate

    although above the water is a rectangle of black

sites by the soundscape of an approaching train, horns

    if the moon is not in the picture, then

and clacking rapidly vanishing into the distance,

    it must be sharing the space with the viewer,

and by an imposing oceanscape, matted, framed,

    where consequently this wartime lounge chair

and suspended on the wall, bringing the outdoors in, or

    would be placed, on a deck, a home's or a ship's

the indoors out, as the designer put it, though he meant

supporting this reading as to the moon's placement

something else, non-decorative, and few must've truly lounged

is a shimmering horizon line; as to the chair,

at the airport, USO, and company waiting rooms it first was in

in judging furniture, appearances are per force inconclusive

66 You keep getting lost. To be able to believe what you say, one would continually need to forget what you just said.

LA GRAN SEÑORA

For a real drama in three episodes, the Producer demands that a Script Doctor resolve the following issues:

1) Who is the neighbor?
   Is she loyal to her sick husband?
   Does she help get him killed?
   Is she having a fling at the hospital?

2) Are there coyotes in the south border?
   Were they startlingly satiated?
   Are they the bad actors?

3) Intimate Confessions?
   Historic Panties
   Mortal Illnesses
   Peaks and Pits
   A Dangerous Tunnel
   A Talent Scout's Greed

AD COPY

Language roundabouts that go places, not language about. The mantra of *The Happy End / All Welcome* might be that slapstick speaks louder than words, the work imploding with what it implies.

GUERRILLA ADVERTISER POSITION

Duties include:

1. As usage of commercial cell-phone jammers is illegal in many districts, develop systems circumventing current legislation to disable mobiles and prevent them from receiving signals from base stations.

2. Design forms to interrupt wireless radio signals and jam satellite communications. Some of the more common methods include transmitting the following to the opponent's receiving equipment: atmospheric, random noise; recorded samples of applause, whistling, or laughing; bagpipe-like sounds or howling ones; and signals resembling sparks and the cries of seagulls.

3. Develop ways to hack global positioning systems (GPS) as well as other navigational tools, including Google Maps and iMaps, to reroute users to places better than their original destinations.

4. Tweet liberation slogans and dumbfounding quotes to The Company's followers—no contextual information or authors' names are to be included in the tweets. Examples:

Never give up before it's too late.

To sit is a verb.

The trouble with palliatives is that they become the whole life.

Images are the murder of the present.

Happiness is not always fun.

The fun is foreseeing the unforeseeable and getting screwed anyway.

How does it feel to be a problem?

Mind your wound.

CULTIVATION STRATEGY

Seeking receivers
of the principal substance
offered by a World Wide Web
site once known
as readers willing
and able to gather in groups
of as few as two in physical
locations during off-hours
to witness the oral
delivery of advanced secure
communications,
communications otherwise
bound to devices.
And/or receivers willing and able
to encounter the principal
substance provided in flat
analogue surfaces not notated
with Hypertext Markup Language
one-on-one.

TABLE 22

Slides are projected onto the pages of a large sketchbook on top of a small table. An Architect turned Location Scout looks at images of different cities to which The Company is considering touring. The Producer sits across from her in a far less formidable seat, and while the candidate looks at the projections, fires all kinds of questions:

How does the locus orbis influence the individual and the collective?

What can psychology tell us about the fact that a certain person sees the city in one way while others see it in another?

How does the idler participate in the mechanism of the city without knowing it?

How does one make a scene?

How does the idler share the image of the city?

What is the role of the speculative in the mechanism by which a city grows?

Who are the would-be tourists of a vanished world?

The Architect turned Location Scout produces the following brief.

The name of a city in the distance is one thing. Once we arrive in it, it takes on another name.

Upon arriving in a new city we find a past we did not know we had: in every new place, what we no longer are awaits us.

Any city takes its shape in opposition to flatness. Contrast is an organizing principle.

Yet we move across the streets as we move across written pages: we are summoned, asked to repeat their discourse.

Palimpsest city: the mere name of the urban center contains its whole past in it.

The city contains all the futures once imagined for it, even those that ceased being possible the moment they were imagined.

The more we get lost, the more we understand the logic of the cities we have traveled through before becoming disoriented.

The city is populated by strangers who, upon passing others by, imagine various encounters with them. As soon as their eyes lock, they flee, embarrassed, seeking other strangers as the protagonists of their daydreams.

Here there are only departures, no returns.

The moods of those successively contemplating the city give it different shapes; impossible to know which of its facets is truer than the others.

The city is defined by its incongruities. Random has become the new normal, and normalcy, the exception.

Here people live with less uncertainty than the inhabitants of other cities; they are convinced that the network supporting them is provisional.

In the plazas the same conversations that have been taking place for years continue to go on—the exchanges are exactly the same. It's the participants in the conversations who keep being replaced.

The most common transaction in the city is the exchange of memories.

Upon arriving in the city everything we have ever imagined about it will be overwritten.

City with no depth. Verso and recto, a sheet of paper with a figure on each side: they're inextricable, yet invisible to each other.

The city's daily upkeep leaves a definitive trace in its wake: yesterday's detritus piled up on top of the day-before-yesterday's detritus, and so on.

Why is there no end to the building of the city?

Because its destruction keeps getting postponed.

I heart NY.

66 Every city is citation, cities.

TABLE 35

ARTISTIC DIRECTOR:

Do you have any previous experience?

APPLICANT:

A former self dealt with my unfinished business.

ARTISTIC DIRECTOR:

Did you work at an office?

APPLICANT:

I am very diligent when there is no need to do anything.

ARTISTIC DIRECTOR:

Do you have any skills?

APPLICANT:

I wanted to have them once.

ARTISTIC DIRECTOR:

Define yourself.

APPLICANT:

A very strategic, enterprising procrastinator.

ARTISTIC DIRECTOR:

So, you've got inventory?

APPLICANT:

Catalogues of incompletes.

ARTISTIC DIRECTOR:

So no skills, eh?

APPLICANT:

Not yet.

ARTISTIC DIRECTOR:

I see you're a flaw exaggerator. Works for me too.

APPLICANT:

I guess.

ARTISTIC DIRECTOR:

Admitted.

APPLICANT:

When can I start?

ARTISTIC DIRECTOR:

Right away, my good man.

APPLICANT:

Amazing. I'll go to Oklahama.

ARTISTIC DIRECTOR:

Oklahoma.

(Both sing along.)

Oh, what a beautiful mornin'!

Oh, what a beautiful day!

I've got a beautiful feelin'

Everything's goin' my way.

ADD A MISSING PLACE TO GOOGLE MAPS

On Calle Oklahoma—a short street in the Neapolitan neighborhood of Mexico City, where streets are named after the American Union's states—an imposing institutional building looms, as well as two other noteworthy ones:

> A. Between Nebraska and Montana, across from where a Coca-Cola truck seems perpetually parked, the Federal Commission for the Protection of Sanitary Risks.

> B. Between Indiana and Pennsylvania, the Human Rights Commission.

> C. Between Pennsylvania and New York, the School for Mechanical and Electrical Engineering.

The rest is low-rises and parking lots, due to the street's proximity with Mexico's version of the World Trade Center.

The Company considers dispatching personnel to all three buildings, but not before researching what occupies the efforts of the state employees in building A.

"They're busy taking miracle products off the market," a member of the translation task force relays. "You know, supposed medicines claiming to relieve stress, cause weight loss, burn fat, regain lost hair. Slim grass, artichoke pills, that sort of thing."

SEEKING

Naturopaths to cure nonspecific symptoms.
Group polarizers.
Encryptors and motivational speakers
to attack The Hostile Network, form mesh-like others.

VIEW FROM A MONOBLOC CHAIR

The Furniture Tester admits that she has been so absorbed in filing her reports and minding logistical details, she had failed to take note of the everyman's outdoor chair: the Monobloc.

So ubiquitous it is that the inventor of the pop-up ad has praised it for being one of the very few "context-free objects" in the world.

It's the plastic.

Upon reflection, it dawns on her that the Monobloc has likely been a witness to The Company's comings and goings, to their socializing on the street, at markets, sidewalk cafés and bars, and perhaps to some of its street performances as well.

The Monobloc welcomes all.

Bearing no trademark, it can be seen all over the web in locations from the shores of the Golden Horn in Istanbul to senior homes in Pensacola, Florida; from food stands in Panamanian markets and tree-shaded areas in Cape Verdean streets to beaches in Croatia; from Pakistani playgrounds to Ukraine's war-torn streets and Jerusalem's Western Wall; from a cultural center in Fortaleza, Brazil, to a museum gallery in New York City, stacked to form the pedestal of a shiny sculpture resembling a pool toy.

She tries to compute how many times she must have sat in one, and realizes it's the kind of thing you're bound to ignore unless it's in the wrong place. Say, indoors.

It seems like yesterday when she spotted a couple of
Monoblocs at a table where people had left signs of preferring
Scrabble over texting or browsing the internet while sitting
around.

TABLE 28

IDHSELZ

PFMORRE

UTNTLIO

BNAAANS

UTTFIAW

WKEDYAE

BKSENDU

ELIRUSE

At the edge of the field, there's a hunting blind and watchtower.

In the first stand former members of the Headhunters band;
in the second, a female border patrol officer. When they're not
encouraging migrants to cross over into the fairgrounds, they are
contemplating the upper regions of the sky, cataloguing clouds.

66 You're educated and must have beautiful handwriting, so you could make a list of everything we have.

PARTIAL INVENTORY

Quante poltrone diverse avete visto nella vostra vita?

Afro-futurist throne made from repurposed wood, with bands
of red, orange, green, and gold recalling a Pan-African flag.

Armchair marrying ergonomics and visual lightness named
after saint.

Assertively wonky inside-out armchairs. No upholstery hides
their armature. They revel in their misshapenness and appear
on the verge of collapse, only optically.

Bistro chair and mid-century modern school chair around
three-legged coffee table.

Pair of chairs, one carefully balanced atop the other, about to
fall and precipitate a chemical or physical reaction.

Chairs made mostly of air between bent steel rods. Unbent and
activated by touch, these rods make ambient music.

Chairs rid of their prosthetic and bodily appearance forming
pragmatic inhabitable sculptures.

Chair thrown out the window by a poet.

Cushioned lounge chair that springs back to original form as
soon as sitter gets up from it.

Dentist chair, nonfunctional.

Desk lying sideways on the ground, bottom wood panels displaying collection of ashtrays from hotels and restaurants alongside commemorative plates.

Egg chair.

Egg and butter chair.

Ergonomic kneeling chair on wheels.

Exaggeratedly long table with small veneer barrier dividing it in half, as if designed for a tabletop game in which opponents should avoid seeing cards each of them are dealt.

Grasshopper chair.

Gray plexiglass table in the shape of footprint, with additional layer of plexiglass on top for photos to be placed underneath.

Group of performance work chairs, formerly known as office chairs.

Hanging rattan chair facing classic bentwood chair.

Idea of a chair that isn't a chair.

Improvised desk with door for a top, with hole in the middle due to missing glass panels.

Inscrutable valet chair.

Knockoff cane chair paired with knockoff Tanker steel desk.

Luxury favela chair.

Mahogany wing chair with tufted leather padding and overly tall back. Scroll wings flanking head area all the way to the arm rests to give sitter privacy, protection from drafts, and support if falling asleep.

Metallic lifeguard chair facing wooden lifeguard chair.

Minimalist chair whose art "is partly its reasonableness, usefulness, and scale as a chair."

Modernist chair derived from "the better camping and military chairs of the nineteenth century."

Modernist chair that is "an almost forgivable sentimentalizing of the machine."

Multiple seats displaying the manifold ways in which single chrome tubes can be bent.

Neon tubes intersecting to form alternate version of electric chair.

Nineteen sixty-eight student-movement anti-design statement against strictures and corporatization of modern design—that celebration of the body commonly known as the beanbag chair—behind a curved L-shape teak desk.

One hundred chairs improvised daily and assembled mostly

from parts of found chairs.

Pair of airplane seats spray-painted in plaid.

Pair of astronaut chairs with lighting umbrellas over them circling on carousel surrounding sculpture of fried egg.

Pair of sunbleached deckchairs.

Ribbons of bentwood forming chair that pays homage to the sturdiness of apple crates once associated with childhood.

Rocker facing a tandem bench with red, yellow, and blue seats.

Séance table displaying the legend "Connected Through Harmony Matter" in Dutch.

Scraps of plywood shoddily nailed together to provide seating.

Stackable ant-like chair made of laminated layers of veneer, inspiration for highest number of knockoffs in modern history and subject of aggressive stomping from fabricators to prove the original's durability.

Surrealist piece with missing seat on whose structure rests an orthopedic hip brace, straps and twine dangling down chair's legs, along with a strip of wax resembling barnacles or fungus.

Table covered in Astroturf.

Table standing empty at edge of stream.

Table for man without qualities.

Teak desk surrounded by late 1800s double-width dining chair and generic, gray office chair upholstered in fried egg fabric, sunny-side up.

Teatro Chair, a heavy, hard-angled red chair designed by urban theorist, placed atop a small stage.

Telephone chair.

Two adult-size chairs behind modern two-person school desk. An Underwood typewriter and a geometrical wooden prop, painted in black and in the shape of a lamp, on desktop.

Assistant Director *(into megaphone)*:

Gooooooooooooooooooooooal!

OK, THIS IS IT

We cannot tell you what it is because we don't have a definition for it.

Defining it would be as ludicrous as attempting to list the attributes of cloud formations worth looking at. While busying ourselves with enumerating them, the shapes would've already changed.

You might be thinking, Why not take pictures then? Surely they would come in handy!

Our reply, "Yes, flatten and section the sky into rectangles! And throw in the earth as well!"

See, for us, it could be objects.

Odd chairs.

An egg or a dream.

Pictures on canvas or screens.

Jazz funk. A soccer match.

A protest. A sitcom.

We arrived here not knowing where we were headed.

We followed contradictions and our intuition (carefully calibrating randomness).

Do not be like us. That would defeat our purpose.

We seek marginal fame.

We do not want followers.

We like to make friends but not to influence people.

We are outsiders to most and anomalies to many.

Our waffling and dithering short-circuits quantification.

Our attentions cannot be captured.

Our opinions have shifting targets.

Our sentiments cannot be measured.

We don't want to win you over.

We don't know what this is and that is why we like it.

Some will object and say, "This is not it!"

So what. Most of it isn't even ours.

Like "A New Career in a New Town," this was made but it wasn't written.

The next one up is in made-up tongues.

Acknowledgments

Some of the language in the poems has been culled from various
sources, including Kafka's *Amerika: The Man Who Disappeared*,
translated by Michael Hofmann, as well as Mark Harman's version
Amerika: The Missing Person. Additional sources include, but are
not limited to, interviews and writings by Martin Kippenberger,
Mechanical Turk, typing manuals, Bruno Munari's *Seeking comfort in an
uncomfortable chair*, Herman Miller promotional material, Donald Judd's
essay "It's Hard to Find a Good Lamp," Aldo Rossi's *The Architecture of
the City*, ghostwritten texts, and blurbs for the books of fellow poets.

Versions of some of these poems appeared in the chapbook *The
Happy End* (The Song Cave, 2014) and the anthology *I'll Drown My
Book: Conceptual Writing by Women,* edited by Caroline Bergvall,
Laynie Brown, Teresa Carmody, and Vanessa Place (Les Figues Press,
2012). "Questionnaire for Prospective Cigarette Tester" appeared in
Imperial Matters; "Table 41" in *Eleven Eleven*; "View from a Folding
Chair" the *New Yorker*; "Describe What Color is Not" was originally
commissioned for the catalogue for *Figuring Color: Kathy Butterly, Felix
Gonzalez-Torres, Roy McMakin, and Sue Williams* (ICA Boston, 2012)
and later published in *Poem-A-Day*; "View from an Aeron Chair" and
"View from a Dodo Chair" in *Poetry*; "The Furniture Tester" appeared
in *Harper's*. An early draft of the poem now titled "The Following
Brief" was written originally in Spanish as a response to Diana Garza
Islas's *Fin de cita* (Lenguaraz, 2010). The four poems following "Table
7" were written for the book accompanying the exhibition *Xul Solar
and Jorge Luis Borges: The Art of Friendship* (Americas Society,
2013). The poems "Blue," "Yellow," and "Red" were written at Suzanne
McClelland's invitation to respond to her exhibition *Put Me in the
Zoo* at Sue Scott Gallery in 2009. Audio recordings of these poems
are archived in Manuel Cirauqui's §ympo§ium on Wave Farm.

My thanks go to these publications' editors and those whose friendship and support made this work possible: Mary Jo Bang, Manuel Cirauqui, Alan Felsenthal and Ben Estes, Robert Fitterman, Alan Gilbert, Ben Lerner, Wendy Lotterman, Suzanne McClelland, Gabriela Rangel, Kim Rosenfield, Sabine Russ, Jeremy Sigler, Betsy Sussler, Matvei Yankelevich and everyone at Ugly Duckling Presse, Lila Zemborain, and most especially, the Lannan Foundation, for a generous residency in Marfa, Texas that made it possible to focus exclusively on the manuscript at a time when it would have been impossible to do otherwise. To Bruce my deepest gratitude, always.